What Dangerous Men Tell Gullible Women

IN·THE·CHURCH

W/ Love,
Your Sister
Kaiuk K. Daniels

What Dangerous Men Tell Gullible Women
IN·THE·CHURCH

KANIKA KATHERINE DANIELS

VANTAGE Press

Cover design by Sheila Hart Design, Inc.

Vantage Press and the Vantage Press colophon are registered trademarks of Vantage Press, Inc.

FIRST EDITION

All rights reserved, including the right of reproduction in whole or in part in any form.

Copyright © 2012 by Kanika Katherine Daniels

Published by Vantage Press, Inc.
419 Park Ave. South, New York, NY 10016

Manufactured in the United States of America
ISBN: 978-0-533-16373-1

Library of Congress Catalog Card No: 2010904917

0 9 8 7 6 5 4 3 2 1

Dedication

To all who want to love, are loving and will love.

WHAT DANGEROUS MEN TELL GULLIBLE WOMEN
IN·THE·CHURCH

Contents

INTRODUCTION
11

PART ONE
13

ABOUT LOVE
25

ABOUT LIFE
45

ABOUT FAMILY
57

Introduction

In this little book, you will learn about some unknown facts about life and love from Scriptures of the Bible. Examples include information on the roles in marriage, how to discipline children, and whether Mary the mother of Jesus was actually a saint or not. Questions that have been lingering for centuries will be answered in detail, through the Word.

The inspiration for this book is two-fold. The first thought of inspiration comes from my life as a Christian, pushed and lured to speak out against the injustice false prophets created in many congregations. The second is a positive recollection of all of the love and wisdom He gives. It glorifies Him as a deliverer, healer and lover. This book is my testimony to the world that God is still alive, has power and does care.

To everyone, Christian or (not yet), this volume is geared toward enlightening everyone's senses when tackling some of the misunderstandings, and outright lies that plague the minds of those, wanting to know God, have relations or communion with Him. This next passage of scripture from 2 Timothy 3:13-15 is a focal point, because this book helps guard us against these wrong elements. The inspiration for this book was first kindled by it.

> 13 But evil men and impostors will grow worse and worse, deceiving and being deceived. 14 But you must continue in the things which you have learned and been assured of, knowing from whom you have learned them, 15 and that from

childhood you have known the Holy Scriptures, which are able to make you wise for salvation, through faith which is in Christ Jesus.

2 Timothy 3 is a great chapter to read in the Bible. It describes the raw man and raw woman, in that it describes how we are without God in our lives. It speaks of dangerous men and gullible women, who are the kind of people we encounter on a daily basis. The evil men, this passage of Scripture describes, are non-Christian men and the impostors include women.

Every time we read God's Words, we are reassured that love will prevail. God is not oblivious to the sorrows we face, in these treacherous times. Nothing is new under the sun and just as God has delivered the Saints of old, He has just enough power to deliver us. The Word of God placed in this book is a guide.

Enjoy reading *What Dangerous Men Tell Gullible Women*. I believe this book is for everyone who is interested in learning facts they've never heard before. It is for everyone, because the Bible has the answers to all of life's concerns. This is the kind of knowledge that stops divorces, blesses and protects children, and makes people believe in love again; because God is love. Bless you.

was because they started having impure thoughts of each other, because of the awareness they gained. Before, it was okay that they were naked; their skin was their clothing.

> 8 And they heard the sound of the Lord God walking in the Garden, in the cool of the day, and Adam and his wife hid themselves from the presence of the Lord God, among the trees of the Garden.

EXPLANATION: Because of their newly found awareness, they knew they were in trouble, and foolishly thought they could hide from the Lord God, in the Garden he created for them.

> 9 Then the Lord God called to Adam and said to him, "Where are you?"

EXPLANATION: When the Lord God asked Adam where he was, it wasn't because He didn't know. It's kind of like a lawyer's sarcasm, because He's asking a question, but He already knows the answer. Some say it's a lawyer's trick, but the Lord God never deceives. It just means that He wants the truth, and nothing but. God is not just a lawyer, but a righteous judge! "Where are you?" is a question that makes Adam think about his state of being. It causes him to think about how close or not close his relationship with the Lord is, at the time. The question is not focused on the literal, but spiritual. It has to do with the state of heart, mind, and soul. The woman was the one who ate the fruit first, but Adam was the first one to sin. The difference in the way the Lord God treats the man and woman, is the difference in their understanding, at the time of deception. Adam knew better; he was not deceived, the woman was.

Adam was the first born, and knew the ramifications of his actions, but did not have the "backbone" or gall to say no, and not eat of the fruit of the Tree of Knowledge of Good and Evil.

> 10 So, he said, "I heard Your voice in the Garden, and I was afraid, because I was naked, and I hid myself." 11 And He said, "Who told you that you were naked? Have you eaten from the tree of which I commanded you that you should not eat?" 12 Then the man said, "The woman whom You gave to be with me, she gave me of the tree, and I ate."

EXPLANATION: Instead of owning up to his sin, the first thing Adam does is blame. Not only is he blaming the woman, but he blames the Lord God, for making her. He does not realize that it was up to him to say no and not eat of the seedless fruit. He also does not comprehend that the woman was made from his body, and not anyone else's. He oversteps his boundaries when he starts to blame God! In our modern day, we see the theme; when a man sins, a woman is blamed. Spiritually speaking, a woman is the body of a man, so when he blames her, he's really blaming himself. The error occurs in the aim of the punishment. (Note of hope: Through Jesus, though, a remnant of men are saved. They inherit the Kingdom of Heaven.) When the Lord God saw the depth of Adam's denial, He confronted the woman.

> 13 And the Lord God said to the woman, "What is this you have done?" The woman said, "The serpent deceived me, and I ate."

Part One

Before going into the questions and answers, we need to know what went wrong with men and women, at the beginning of humankind, in the Garden of Eden. Genesis 3 is written in whole, along with explanations of each verse. It will give a breakdown of those historic events. This will aid in understanding the problems men and women have with communication. This is from the New King James version.

> Now the serpent was more cunning than any beast of the field, which the Lord God had made. And he said to the woman, "Has God indeed said 'You shall not eat of every tree of the Garden?' 2 And the woman said to the serpent, "We may eat the fruit of the trees of the Garden; 3 but of the fruit of the tree which is in the midst of the Garden, God has said, 'You shall not eat it, nor shall you touch it, lest you die.'

EXPLANATION: The serpent in this story is the devil, himself. He is targeting the one who has less understanding of the Word the Lord God, Yahweh, has said.

> 4 Then the serpent said to the woman, "You will not surely die. 5 For God knows that in the day you eat of it, your eyes will be opened, and you will be like God, knowing good and evil."

EXPLANATION: The devil lied when he told her that she won't die, but he didn't lie when explaining that her eyes would be opened, and would be like God. When he said that her eyes would be opened, it meant that she would realize more, and understand good and evil. Like a good liar, he mixed a lie with the truth.

> 6 So, when the woman saw that the tree was good for food, and it was pleasant to the eyes, and a tree desirable to make one wise, she took of its fruit and ate. She also gave to her husband, and he ate. 7 Then the eyes of both of them were opened, and they knew that they were naked, and they sewed fig leaves together, and made themselves coverings.

EXPLANATION: There were three reasons the woman ate of the tree of the knowledge of good and evil. I want to focus on the third reason, which had to do with gaining wisdom. She could quote Scripture but did not understand it; she was vulnerable in the matter. Wisdom was something she didn't have, and was tempted by the serpent to get. Adam was the first human, created before the woman, and had better understanding of the Word the Lord God had given, but even he didn't say no! If he had said no and not eaten the seedless fruit, the world would be totally different; we might still be in the Garden. (Confirmation of the guilt of Adam is found in Romans 5:12-14.) When Eve ate of the seedless fruit, nothing happened, but when Adam ate, there was trouble. After they both ate of the fruit from the forbidden tree, in the midst of the Garden, both of their eyes were opened, and they knew they were naked. The awareness they didn't have they got, but at a terrible price. The reason they made themselves coverings

EXPLANATION: When the Lord God asked the woman what she had done, it is because He understands that she is the action. She is the "body" of Adam. Because the woman has now gained wisdom, He knows that she knows where she is. She was not aware of her own actions, and what they meant before, but now she knows. In that newfound knowledge, she rightly admits that she was deceived by the serpent. She never blames the Lord God or Adam, but tells the truth.

> 14 So, the Lord God said to the serpent, "Because you have done this, you are cursed more than all cattle, and more than every beast of the field; on your belly you shall go, and you shall eat dust, all the days of your life.

EXPLANATION: When the Lord God sees and hears the woman's confession, He knows that she is telling the truth, and turns to confront the serpent, to curse him. Before giving judgment on the man and woman, the Lord God deals with the serpent first, because he caused the first temptation, and targeted the "weakest link." The serpent's lie caused a deadly chain of reaction.

> 15 And I will put enmity between you and the woman, and between your seed and her Seed; He shall bruise your head, and you shall bruise His heel."

EXPLANATION: With enmity or ill will, the serpent or devil, is forever angry at the woman for telling on him. She "dimed" him out! She was a snitch. It also explains the fact that women are more aware, because of the gaining of wisdom, and shows the loss of wisdom, men have gained. God does not say that there is enmity between man and the serpent, but between the woman and the serpent. The serpent used the naive woman to get to the man, but now he's using the simple man, to get to the woman. Ten percent will survive this spiritual warfare, thank God! In this passage of Scripture, we are also introduced to Jesus. "Her Seed" is the intro; and it gives us a preview of the fact that God would send His son on earth, in the flesh, to save us from our sin, and claim His "bride." And, "He shall bruise your head, and you shall bruise his heel," gives us a glimpse of the crucifixion Jesus underwent. One of the things that Jesus went through had to do with the medical aspect of the physical death. In a medical report of Jesus, we learn that fluid was building up in Jesus' lungs, and He had to push Himself up, while on the cross, to drain some of the fluid, so He could breathe. He had to use His heels to do it. So even before Jesus is born on the earth, Genesis describes His physical death.

> 16 To the woman He said, "I will greatly multiply your sorrow and your conception; In pain you shall bring forth children; Your desire shall be for your husband, And he shall rule over you."

EXPLANATION: When He says the sorrow will be multiplied, it means wisdom. Solomon said it when he said much wisdom brings much grief, (Ecclesiastes 1:18). The discernment Adam had was switched over to the woman. The awareness that she acquired from the fruit, makes her aware of pain, something that was not so in the beginning. When having a child, every woman has her own level of awareness. This means if she is very wise, she has more pain than other women, who are less wise. Of course, through Jesus, a woman is able to get through anything. Because Adam had lost his awareness, it is natural that women seem to be the great thinkers. "Your desire shall be for your husband," means that women will have a tendency to have to make decisions for their husbands. When we look at the state of the world, and we see women starving themselves, wearing makeup, every day, doing bikini waxes, putting deadly chemicals on their hair and lips, etc., we see what the Scripture is saying, when it says, ". . .and he shall rule over you." Many of these things are hazardous to a woman's health, but are done anyway. All of these terrible things that women go through were not designed by God, but by man. If you notice, what the Lord God says is not a curse. Initially, God blessed the man and the woman and He did not take it back! The things the Lord God says, are not what He wants, but are natural progressions of the eating of the fruit of the tree of the knowledge of good and evil. It was not Eve's fault that sin came into the world, but, of course, her life would have to be altered, because Adam's life was altered; she is his "body." Through Jesus, we are saved even from this. For example, Queen Esther is an example of a woman, who had to disobey her husband, because what he was being led to do, was against her Lord. As Scripture dictates, a woman is only to obey her husband, as is fitting in Christ, not man. If she did obey, she could not call herself a child of God. Both husband and wife are to obey God.

17 Then to Adam He said, "Because you have heeded the voice of your wife, and have eaten from the tree of which I commanded, "You shall not eat of it, cursed is the ground for your sake; in toil you shall eat of it, all the days of your life.

EXPLANATION: "Because you have heeded the voice of your wife," means he was not supposed to listen to someone who did not understand what the consequences were. The woman didn't know, and so the man was obligated to say "no," but he let her down. She actually needed protection for herself, but obviously Adam had his own ulterior motive. We know this, because they have a connection. In this verse, God makes a note of it. Adam is not cursed, but the ground for his sake is. From then on, work will be harder for the man. It's not because he is physically incapable, but it will be harder for him to reason it out, mentally. The trouble he will have will be all in his head; I'm talking confidence or lack of. One of the reasons it's good for a man to have a wife is, for challenge and encouragement; to be better than he thinks. The Bible says, "The man that findeth a wife, findeth a good thing." Every time a man looks at a woman, he is reminded that he needs help! Christian men are the only ones who appreciate this fact, but most men are embittered by it. The curse for both man and woman is a disconnect, but when Jesus died on the Cross, He brought back the connection. If people obey His Word, the communication breakdown will be remedied; there will be no more disconnection. Husband and wife will understand each other, and work well together, again.

> 18 Both thorns and thistles it shall bring forth for you, and you shall eat the herb of the field.
>
> 19 In the sweat of your face you shall eat bread, till you return to the ground, for out of it you were taken; for dust you are, and to dust you shall return."

> 20 And Adam called his wife's name Eve, because she was the mother of all living.
>
> 21 Also for Adam and his wife the Lord God made tunics of skin, and clothed them.

EXPLANATION: This was the first time an animal was killed for mankind's sake. This is why the animals are wary of us. They know what we did because they suffer. Although, of course, we are more valuable than the animals, and through faith in God, we are saved.

> 22 The Lord God said, "Behold, the man has become like one of Us, to know good and evil. And now, lest he put out his hand and take also of the Tree of Life, and eat, and live forever."
> 23 Therefore the Lord God sent him out of the Garden of Eden, to till the ground from which he was taken. 24 So, He drove out the man; and He placed cherubim at the east of the Garden of Eden, and a flaming sword, which turned every way, to guard the way to the tree of Life.

EXPLANATION: The only reason we are all not in the Garden of Eden right now, is because of our newfound knowledge. God did not want to risk us hurting ourselves, again, and eating from the Tree of Life, so man was kicked out. He placed cherubim, meaning angels, and a fiery sword to block our way to it. It would be a mess if we had to deal with our evil ways, forever. God protects us from ourselves. Just imagine if someone had a lung disease, because they smoked cigarettes for most of their life. They committed the sin of defiling their body, and they would have to deal with having breathing problems, forever. It would be agony! It was kind for God to drive them out of the Garden, away from the Tree of Life.

Ever since Adam's sin, men and women have had a breakdown in communication, which has caused a debilitating strain on marriages. As a result of broken homes, the world has lost trust in happiness, through marriage. Most people are not satisfied, and some have even made up an 80/20 rule. As was explained to me, some psychologists believe that in marriage you will only get 80 percent of what you need. They use this reasoning to stop people from being adulterous, and taking the 20 percent they might gain from an affair. The point is, that the people who made up the 80/20 rule, don't even believe they can get 100 percent satisfaction from their marriage; they think they can get only 80 percent! That is a falsehood about marriage in itself, because it limits love. God is love and He is not limited! Only a person who does not understand the power of love, would conjure up such a rule. Those psychologists or counselors are confusing love with lust. Because some have never seen happy marriages in their family, they really don't see the relevance of marriage. They grew up with a single parent, and think that it should be considered as normal. Through the Word of God, we will see why it should not be considered as normal. Marriage is important in sustaining balance in society. Without it, we get worse, and worse, and the anger brought on by the lack of trust in love, will build. Thank God we have an outlet that gives hope and restores love back into the family.

Enjoy reading *What Dangerous Men Tell Gullible Women*, and now, we are ready for more information coming from God's Word. It is powerful and sweet, clearing up a lot of confusion. Now we are ready for the questions and answers section. It's important to start out right, learning the basics of the Christian belief. Enjoy!

About Love

1 **WHY IS PRE-MARITAL SEX BAD?**
Answers: 1–Thessalonians 4:1-8; 1 Corinthians 5:9-13; 1 Peter 2:11-12; Acts 15:20 (New King James Version); Proverbs 5 and 7; 2 Timothy 3.

1 THESSALONIANS 4:1-8 *Finally then, brethren, we urge and exhort in the Lord Jesus that you should abound more, and more, just as you received from us how you ought to walk, and to please God; 2 For you know what commandments we gave you through the Lord Jesus. 3 For this is the will of God, your sanctification: that you should abstain from sexual immorality; 4 that each of you should know how to possess his own vessel, in sanctification and honor. 5 Not in passion of lust, like the Gentiles, who do not know God; 6 that no one should take advantage of and defraud his brother in this matter, because the Lord is the avenger of all such, as we also forewarned you, and testified. 7 For God did not call us to uncleanness, but in holiness. 8 Therefore he who rejects this, does not reject man, but God, who has also given us His Holy Spirit.*

1 PETER 2:11-12 *"Beloved, I beg you as sojourners and pilgrims, abstain from fleshly lusts, which war against the soul, 12 having your conduct hon-*

orable among the Gentiles, that when they speak against you as evildoers, they may, by your good works, which they observe, glorify God, in the day of visitation."

1 CORINTHIANS 5:9-13 "I wrote to you in my epistle not to keep company with sexually immoral people. 10 Yet I certainly did not mean with the sexually immoral people of this world, or with the covetous, or extortioners, or idolaters, since then you would need to go out of the world. 11 But now I have written to you, not to keep company with anyone named a brother, who is sexually immoral, or covetous, or an idolater, or a reviler, or a drunkard, or an extortioner—not even to eat with such a person. 12 For what have I to do with judging those, also who are outside? Do you not judge those who are inside? 13 But those who are outside, God judges. Therefore, put away from yourselves the evil person."

Related Scriptures:
PROVERBS 31:11-12 "The heart of her husband safely trusts her; so he will have no lack of gain. 12 She does him good and not evil, all the days of her life."

EXPLANATION: The consequences of pre-marital sex are related to the problem of conditional love. Conditional love is not love. Proverbs 31:1-3 warns men on not giving their strength to women and definitely warns women to respect themselves and not be the harlot. Five reasons why premarital sex is bad include: men not being trustworthy, women manipulating with their bodies, neglected and abused children, cancer, and the impact on society.

The first reason why pre-marital sex is bad has to do with men not being trustworthy or love-accountable. The reason he has no trust in women is, because he has no trust in himself. It is not a woman's fault that a man has no trust, but it has to do with his unresolved issues, of not understanding how to lead. The reason men have trouble committing, starts with the childhood trauma of not seeing his father trusting his mother. He does not have guidance from his parents in finding the right wife. In most cases, the boy is being raised by a single mother, or an overbearing, unloving father. Some people think that marriage is not relevant, but without it, children don't see trust between their parents. Their father does not trust the mother with his heart; meaning, his feelings and attention. The boy is not seeing his father obeying his mother. Later in this book, you will read how the husband is in charge of cooking for his wife, but also in Ephesians 5:29, the husband is to cherish his wife. Cherish means, to keep in mind. A Christian man understands that women need help with physical things; the Bible makes certain to mention that husbands are responsible for love, also. There is a difference between a sperm donor, and a real father. Fathers are there for their children; the sperm donor makes excuses, and is not there. Sperm donors, or immoral men, are not real men, in the eyes of God.

A man who won't commit in marriage, is a man who does not love. His commitment is only to lust. He's not trying to trust his heart to a woman. It means that something is wrong; an anger or sorrow that has not been resolved.

The man who has pre-marital sex, is a man who has trust issues. Some men say that if a woman does not have sex with them, that she is showing no trust. Men who say this, are definitely men who do not know how to lead. A rule of thumb about men is, in order for them to get respect they have to give it first. It is not the job of the woman to lead. Other men say that she's being a tease. When a woman obeys God, she can never be a tease! The whole point of obedience to God is love, not deception. Another reason some men make excuses for not obeying God, has to do with laziness. Love is work. Effort has to be put into love, because it involves serving. These men always think they should get something for nothing! Because they blame women, including their mothers, for all of their problems, they believe that a woman owes them; they think the whole world owes them. The fact that Christian women are not giving up on the notion that a man could actually love, is a compliment to men. The immoral woman is the one who has given up on love, and enables men to do evil. They only think they will be loved for what they do, and not for who they are. 1 Thessalonians chapter 4 speaks of this deception, or fraud. Their futures are full of trouble. How a man tricks a woman into having sex, and in doing other kinds of sin is, he makes her feel sorry for him. (The reference on men tricking women is 2 Timothy 3:1-9.) He accuses her of the very thing he is guilty of, and she is foolish enough to believe it! The main thing that they do, is accuse women of not caring. You have to remember, the way a man accuses a woman is how he accuses God. There is a connection between women and God, in that God gave women to be a gift for men. God loves men so much that

He gave every good thing to them. This is one of the reasons that sex before marriage is a sin, and becomes evil in the sight of God, because they don't trust Him to wait, and be married, first. There is a lack of love. Of course, if the immoral repent of their sins, by apologizing to each other and please God by getting married, the sin is gone.

Secondly, when a woman has pre-marital sex, it means she is trying to manipulate a man. When she does this, it means she doesn't think he will ever love her, unless she does it. Even if she gets a man to marry her this way, it will end up backfiring, and she will be miserable. Some miserable situations include: adultery, verbal and physical abuse. In most cases it ends up in divorce, because the couple started off with a lack of trust. It's not totally about trusting people, but about trusting God, to work through the tough times. A woman should never feel obligated to give away her virginity in order to keep a man. Sex should not be taken lightly. Even if one does not become pregnant or diseased, the person is spiritually and emotionally broken; there is a loss of self-worth. The problem is that some women think if a man says he doesn't want sex, she automatically accuses him of not thinking she's beautiful, or accuses him of being gay. On the contrary, if a man is obeying God, he can never think that a woman is not beautiful; the Bible says that women of God are the glory, and true Christian men are not gay. The reason true Christian men are not gay is because the homosexual lifestyle shows conditional love. Their love is only based on what they can do for each other, not for who they are. Their feelings of inadequacy with the opposite sex fuel their isolation. This falls into self-hatred because they are not fulfilling their true and optimal potential. Most women think that if a man has sex with her, it means he loves her, but that's not true, unless there is a commitment through marriage. They end up finding out the hard way! Men need help understanding love, because of the Genesis experience and sin that was committed; at the moment, the woman is being seen only as an object, not an equal partner or person. An example of this is oral sex. Some women allow men to take away their dignity, by making them do things with their mouth that are not proper or sanitary. She is not real in his life. Even though he is not rejecting the sex, many men lose trust in women, who have pre-marital sex. It shows in most men, because they end up being unsure of marriage, when a woman starts demanding a love commitment, which can only be accomplished through a sound marriage. Most men understand that if she was easily coaxed to have sex with him, she could easily be persuaded by another man. She ends up being passed around, for temporary satisfaction. Because so many women think that men have the same learning style, they end up being foolish.

The learning style has to do with a woman knowing how to demand love from a man. The only way a woman can gain respect from a man is through her conduct (1 Peter 3:1-2). Words are for women, pictures are for men. Women think first, and act second, men act first, and think second. If a man has never seen love between his parents, he does not know how to love a woman. So if she abstains from sex before marriage, it lets him know right away that she is different. She is not the harlot, like the majority of women of the world. (Only a remnant or 10 percent of the world's population is going to Heaven, because of the

Genesis experience, (Romans 11:5). Women need to understand that virginity is precious, and it is power. God's way is always better.

The main point is that if you want a bright and healthy future, it's better to obey God, and not take such a serious risk with your life. Every true Christian understands that man-made things break. Condoms, Norplant, the "pill" are examples of things that will never be 100 percent effective and unharmful.

When a woman shows the heart of not wanting to manipulate, God also protects her from being raped. A woman can't protect herself from being ravaged, but if she has her heart on the loving ways of Jesus, she will be protected by God, Himself. Deciding to be wise and not foolish is important. She has to love herself properly. Because, why would God protect her, if she thinks she knows how to protect herself? It is the same with a man, if he thinks he knows better than God! God only takes care of His children, not the devil's.

The third reason pre-marital sex is bad, revolves around the neglect and abuse of children. The children suffer when their parents break up, because fathers were not trustworthy, and mothers were manipulative. The reason we have criminal gangs, prostitution, drug abuse, and murders, because of the broken homes created, when people are irresponsible. They value lust over love. The temporary "fix" of lust will not keep a happy home. It only causes anger and grief. Children become unwanted. Some women say that they are financially capable of raising a child, but the point is sanity; are the children sane? Whenever the mother looks at her child, she will be forever reminded of the man, who broke her heart, and vice versa for single father, who are angry at women. We see this when mothers are reported putting their babies in the trash. Men are the leaders in the family, or "heads," so for some women, just like the man abandoned them, they follow his lead, and do these horrible things. Because he gives up, they give up! They're called evil by God, because they are not demonstrating love, but selfishness.

The fourth problem has to do with our physical health. Medical statistics show that women who have multiple sexual partners, are at a higher risk of developing cervical cancer. People have to understand that there is a connection between the spiritual, and the physical. Obeying God, actually prevents cancer! Most people would not want to realize that the lack of love, actually causes illnesses, but the statistics show, how the epidemic has grown. Nowadays, there's even a vaccine for HPV that is supposed to help fight it, but of course, we know that man-made things, only make things worse. The drug only causes more health issues for women. Some are deadly. Obeying the Word of God, is the true cure for cervical cancer.

Lastly, having pre-marital sex has a bad impact on society. With so many broken hearts in the world, with men not knowing how to love their families, and women accepting lust over love, we are in trouble. Some say they can take care of their children, without a husband, and others say they are better off, without a wife. To answer those statements, they might be financially stable enough to take care of their children, but the problem is sanity. Will their children be sane or spiritually balanced? Examples of spiritual things include love, anger, grief, despair, happiness, etc. The terrible anxiety caused by the lack of love in families, is very apparent. The reason we have criminal gangs is, because children are searching for a family. Of course, we see how deceived they are, because the love they get is conditional. If they sell drugs, beat someone up, or rape a woman, they will be loved and given respect, but it's not real. They don't know the difference because they've never seen love. The lack of love causes their minds to be totally debased. They're totally out of control! To create the best situation for children, marriage before sex is the best. In order for a man to be a good father, he has to be a good husband, first; vice versa for women. The only way to have peace of mind is through Jesus. He is our example for living. The whole Bible is focused on Him, and His way to salvation. He protects us from ourselves, if we let Him.

2. What does it mean for a man to love his wife, and a woman to obey her husband?

Answers: Ephesians 5:21-33; Luke 22:24-27; Mark 10:35-45; Colossians 3:18-19.

> EPHESIANS 5:21 *"Submitting to one another in the fear of God."*
>
> EPHESIANS 5:23 *"For the husband is head of the wife, as also Christ is head of the church; and He is the Savior of the body."*
>
> COLOSSIANS 3:18-19 *"Wives, submit yourselves unto your own husbands, as it is fit in the Lord.*

19 Husbands, love your wives, and be not bitter against them." (King James Version)

RELATED SCRIPTURES:

LUKE 22:24-27 "Now there Was also a dispute among them, as to which of them should be considered the greatest. 25 And He said to them, 'The kings of the Gentiles exercise lordship over them, and those who exercise authority over them, are called benefactors. 26 But not so among you; on the contrary, he who is greatest among you, let him be as the younger, and he who governs, as he who serves. 27 For who is greater, he who sits at the table, or he who serves? Is it not he who sits at the table? Yet I am among you as the One who serves.' "

GENESIS 1:27 "So, God created man in His own image; in the image of God He created him; male and female, He created them."

We see through Scripture that God is actually not sexist, favoring men over women, but God loves and protects all who are His children, those who believe in Him. When both husband and wife obey God, they will in safety be able to submit to each other. Because the husband is the "head," spiritually, it means that he obeys first. It is the same when Jesus was courting the Church; the Church is made up of individuals, who believe in what He preached. The Church couldn't obey Jesus, until He obeyed first. (1 John 4:19) The Jews prayed for a King, and God heard their prayers, delivering the Savior, Jesus. He showed love by submitting to the Church, who needed him. The husband is to mimic that love toward his wife. Without love there is suffering. The "body" is the wife, spiritually. While the husband represents the mind and leads, the wife represents the main part of the being, and they create a family. She represents the heart, along with the other important "organs of the body." Both husband and wife are dependent on one another.

When you love someone, you serve them. That is what Jesus does for all who believe, and obey Him. When the Bible speaks on the husband being the "head," it means he is the servant. (Luke 22 and Mark 10) Just like God is the author and Jesus is the finisher of our faith, men are spiritually authors, and women are finishers. Husbands either start something good or something that is bad; constructive or de-constructive. Wives have the choice to finish badly, or do well. Christian men start good things. For example, when a husband starts housework, the wife follows his lead, and helps him to clean.

Leading by example is imperative. Some men think that they are God's gift to all women, but it is actually women who are the gifts, according to the book of Genesis. A woman can't respect her husband until he respects her, first. When men take care of their wives, it is the same as loving God. Men who don't are spiritually and physically slapping God, in the face, saying, "Take your damned gift back! That's dangerous."

3 IN A MARRIAGE RELATIONSHIP, WHO ENDS UP MAKING THE "EXECUTIVE" DECISION?
Answer: The heart ends up making the executive decision, the wife. The mind has questions, but the heart has the

answer. In our lives, we realize that our minds try to figure out the questions we have, but ultimately, it is the heart that gives the final answer. Like some say, "Follow your heart!" Colossians 3, there is a condition on how far a woman would obey her husband. It is contingent on the Lord's standards of living and loving, not on man's standards. Both husband and wife have to be led by God and not by selfishness.

Men control with love, not intellect. If a man wants to have a say in how his wife decides on an issue, he needs to be thorough in how he loves her. The wife always makes her decision, on how she is treated. A couple of examples are: the response some women get when making the decision to change their last names when getting married, and deciding to get hysterectomies to stop their ability to have more children. In the past, there was no question whether a woman would take her husband's last name. But in these days and times, because of the lack of trust associated with love, many women are adding their maiden names to their husband's name, adding a hyphen. They don't want to go through the trouble of paying money to change their names back, it is a protective thing! It is a very bad sign when the woman already feels that she needs to protect herself. Usually, when a marriage starts off wrong, it ends wrong. The same goes for women who make the big decision to not have any more children. When she sees how her husband acts around their first or second child, she chooses this option to protect herself, because she realizes her efforts are not appreciated, or she feels she has to raise her children, and husband; she's tired and weary. Manipulative women are guilty of not telling the truth when they are not comfortable. Here are some related scriptures coming from the King James Version.

MATTHEW 12:35 A good man out of the good treasure of the heart, bringeth forth good things; and an evil man out of the evil treasure, bringeth forth evil things.

MATTHEW 5:8 Blessed are the pure in heart; for they shall see God.

PROVERBS 18:22 Whoso findeth a wife findeth a good thing, and obtaineth favor of the Lord.

4. Is it the place of a woman to be the main cook for her family?
Answer: No. Ephesians 5:28-29.

VERSE 28 "So husbands ought to love their own wives, as their own bodies; he who loves his wife, loves himself.

VERSE 29 "For no one ever hated his own flesh, but nourishes and cherishes it, just as the Lord does the church."

RELATED SCRIPTURE: PROVERBS 12:27
VERSE 27 "The lazy man does not roast what he took in hunting, but diligence is man's precious possession."

Through the Word of God, we see that the husband is responsible for being the main cook. It is one of his duties, as the "head" to lead by example. God calls women helpmates; women help but they are not obligated to lead. According to Scripture, "head" means that the husband leads by serving.

Jesus was the greatest servant. When the husband feeds or nourishes his wife, he also feeds his children, because they derive from her. Of course, as children see their parents being good examples, they follow suit in learning the craft, in order to feed their own families, in the future.

Proverbs 31:14-15 says nothing about a wife cooking, but instead speaks on how she is the personal shopper for the family. She brings her food from afar, and provides food for the household; in other words, she stocks the refrigerator, cabinets, and freezer. The Scripture does not use the word cook, roast, or nourish, in describing the Christian woman, and her duties. Of course, as a survival skill, everyone should be able to cook for themselves.

One of the great things about God's Word for married couples is, it is practical. A man who feeds his wife, helps to keep a peaceful balance in his home. When a woman experiences love from her husband, she will automatically give her husband what he wants. In some cases, it's more sex! When men obey God, it's the best thing! The woman is not forced to carry the whole burden of doing all the household duties. Her husband leads and she follows by helping him. The reason most women are physically ill is, because of this tendency for them to feel obligated to control everything, because the men are not fulfilling their responsibilities. Women are the weaker vessels, meaning weaker in flesh, so when a man leads his wife, she is encouraged, and has peace of mind to give him what he desires. Women want sex, too, but need love to be motivated. Respect and trust is so important, when creating a happy home. If a man obeys God, maintaining his home, a woman has less tension, which reassures her that she is not in the relationship alone. The couple is establishing unwavering trust, which is a big part of love.

Also, we see how God's Word is true, because the best chefs are men, not women. It goes along with a man's talents: being visual and hands on, perfect for most men. The husband's place is in the kitchen, cooking. When men get in their place, women will follow.

5. ARE MEN SUPPOSED TO WORK?
Answer: Yes. 2 Thessalonians 3:6-15.

6 *"Now we command you, brethren, in the name of our Lord Jesus Christ that ye withdraw yourselves from every brother who walketh disorderly, and not after the tradition which he received of us. 7 For yourselves know how ye ought to follow us: for we behaved not ourselves disorderly among you; 8 neither did we eat any man's bread for nought; but wrought with labor and travail, night and day, that we might not be chargeable to any of you: 9 not because we have not power, but to make ourselves an example unto you to follow us. 10 For even when we were with you, this we commanded you, that if any would not work, neither should he eat.*

11 For we hear that there are some who walk among you, disorderly, working not at all, but are busybodies. 12 Now them who are such, we command and exhort by our Lord Jesus Christ, that with quietness they work, and eat

> their own bread. 13 But ye, brethren, be not weary in well doing.
>
> 14 And if any man obey not our word by this epistle, note that men, and have not company with him, that he may be ashamed. 15 Yet count him not as an enemy, but admonish him as a brother."

Paul, the disciple who was inspired by God to write this, is making sure that no one is deceived, or confused about the fact that men are supposed to work. We already know that Christian men work. This is not something I should have to write about, myself, but we see there is still disorder. This should not be confused with men who are laid-off, or are disabled, but for everyone to know that laziness is not supported by God. This passage of Scripture is especially pertinent today, because so many men give excuses for not working. This causes a problem, because the future generation of men will start thinking that they are immuned from having to work; that they cannot work. This world is already being bombarded with this kind of advertisement. Parents should know that they are their children's examples. For most of them, what they see is what they think.

The reason for the disparity has connection with the trouble which happened in Genesis 3. Because of the Genesis experience, mentioned earlier, men have trouble reasoning things out. There is hope in Jesus' Word that this problem can be remedied.

The way this disparity can be resolved is in Proverbs 1:8, where it speaks on sons getting instructions from their fathers, and the law of kindness (Proverbs 31) from their mothers. As long as fathers are not in their place, at home, and married to the mothers of their children, little boys are not getting encouragement. They lack courage to live life to the fullest, with hope and perseverance. Parents need to teach all of their children how to deal with disappointment and to have the discipline to keep moving forward. Parents teach not just by word, but also by deed. The law that mothers teach their sons is the law of kindness. Proverbs 31 speaks on how out of the mouth of the virtuous woman comes wisdom, and on her tongue is the law of kindness. Besides getting instructions from their fathers, boys need wisdom to live by. I've seen too many men quit jobs, because they thought they weren't being respected by the supervisors. The reason other men lose their jobs is because they are not thinking of how that affects the family. They don't even have enough wisdom to wait until they can get a better job. They have no patience! Many employers are prejudiced, for sure, but there is a way to get around that by writing letters, learning your rights, speaking up for yourself. If they had encouragement from their fathers, and wisdom from their mothers, they would not be afraid to communicate. Communication is not bad; it shows intelligence. Men are supposed to work.

6. ARE WOMEN SUPPOSED TO MAKE THEIR OWN MONEY WORKING?

Answer: Yes. Proverbs 31:16, 24.

VERSE 16 *"She considers a field and buys it; from her profits she plants a vineyard."*

VERSE 24 "She makes linen garments and sells them, and supplies sashes for the merchants."

RELATED SCRIPTURE: PROVERBS 13:4
VERSE 4 "The soul of the lazy man desires, and has nothing; but the soul of the diligent shall be made rich."

Love is what opens the mind to see the truth. This portrayal of the virtuous wife/woman is something that all women should strive toward. God has never been sexist; where all of the pressure to make money is on the husband, and He has never been a hater of women; women are allowed to fulfill their dreams. No one has the right, at least biblically, to hold one back from paid work.

Women who believe that God is sexist, will not exactly say it with words, but you will see it through their actions. I've seen some of these women with great careers give them up, in the process of getting married. They gave in to the temptation of disobeying the Bible, because their husbands made so much money, or they were under the notion that God says a woman is supposed to stay home, which they really didn't hear from God, but from an insecure man.

Some women feel tied down by their children. But, it's not just the parents who raise them; it's many others in their circle: family, friends, and "strangers." Times are tough, but here comes a time when people need to trust God. There needs to be a system for taking time with the kids. The important thing to remember, the husband is to lead in raising his children, not the wife.

Women who decide to disobey God, end up being gullible. Their husbands start to control everything they do, and not appreciating them. These men continue to disrespect their wives, because the women are not showing a paycheck; not helping them pay some bills. Those housewives are not comparable to their husbands, like Eve was to Adam. They end up being unequally yoked because, in the Christian world, both husband and wife work, and supply the needs of their family. Also, because the women are not challenging their minds, they end up living vicariously, through their husbands. They end up being an annoying part of their husbands' lives, which can cause problems, later. Of course, things go downhill from there, as they don't allow God's love in. Some men have a tendency to blame their wives if they cheat, even though both of them played a role, in the confusion. It is also important for the wife to show a good example for her children. It's silly to work so hard to finish college and end up a housewife, being vulnerable to the uncontrolled emotional ways of a non-Christian husband. Christian women are trusted by their husbands. The Christian woman helps her husband make money.

About Life

7 **DID EVE BRING SIN INTO THE WORLD?**
Answer: No. Romans 5:12-14.

VERSES 12-14 *"Therefore, just as through one man sin entered the world, and death through sin, and thus death spread to all men, because all sinned—For until the law sin was in the world, but sin is not imputed when there is no law. Nevertheless death reigned from Adam to Moses, even over those who had not sinned, according to the likeness of the transgression of Adam, who is a type of Him who was to come."*

From the mouth of many preachers one hears them rightfully say that Adam was to blame for ushering sin into the world, but women are treated in a way that proves that they blame women. For example, some congregations still do not allow women to preach in their churches, or if they do, they will not ordain them. For others, the only way a woman is ordained, if she is willing to do things the pastor's way, and not God's way; the classic case of the dangerous man, and his group of gullible women. Some are still perpetuating rules that contradict the very nature of God.

According to Genesis 3, when the woman, Eve, ate of the Tree of Knowledge of Good and Evil, nothing happened. Nothing happened, because there was a difference between Adam and Eve. God gave the Word to the man, at that time. When God gives you the Word, it's not just technical, but it includes having wisdom, and understanding. Both wisdom and understanding come from God. Eve could quote Scripture, but that didn't mean she understood it. There's a difference between being able to memorize a word, and actually comprehending its meaning. Initially, Adam was the one who understood the meaning, Eve didn't. Eve understood the technical side of the passage of Scripture, but wisdom and understanding she did not have, at that time. The wisdom and understanding that women have now, did not come until after the Fall of man; it was not her fault. Ironically today, the opposite is true; because of the Genesis experience, women understand the Word of God. Men quote Scripture but they don't understand it until they allow love in, by allowing Christian women to help them. A special example is in the Bible, where it speaks of the male clergy; each having a wife. Some think that it is only to cut off sexual immorality, but we see that they need wives for wisdom. Out of her mouth comes wisdom, and on her tongue is the law of kindness, says Proverbs 31. (Proverbs 8:4-5; 1 Timothy 1:5-7; 2 Timothy 1-9) When speaking of Christian men, in Proverbs there is a passage of Scripture that says that aged men have wisdom. They have to be older to have the wisdom, whereas Christian women have it at a younger age. The heartbreaking part was, when Adam took it upon himself to disobey God. When he ate of the fruit, "all hell broke loose on earth," as some may say. In Genesis, it is also revealed that one of the reasons the fruit of the Tree of Knowledge of Good and Evil was so attractive to Eve, is because it would give her wisdom. Adam knew and understood the Word, but listened to the unknowing woman, anyway. He, in turn, gave up some of his power. Eve needed

Adam to say no, and give confirmation that she was good enough for him. The first test of love, and he failed!

Some of the false preachers say that Eve must have seduced Adam, or tricked him, in some sexual way, into eating the fruit he wasn't supposed to eat. But there's a big problem with that "theory." Adam and Eve didn't even know they were naked, until after Adam ate of the seedless fruit! According to Genesis, chapter 3, God had caught Adam hiding and claiming that he was ashamed because he was naked. God said, "Who told you, you were naked?" No sin or seduction had been introduced, until Adam ate the fruit, not Eve. It was impossible for her to have seduced him. Eve did not bring sin into the world.

8 Does the Pope have the last word?
Answers: No. 1 Timothy 6:15; Numbers 23:19; Isaiah 55:8.

> 1 TIMOTHY 6:14-15 *"That thou keep this commandment without spot, unrebukeable, until the appearing of our Lord Jesus Christ; which in His times He shall shew, who is the blessed and only Potentate, the King of kings, and Lord of lords."*

> NUMBERS 23:19 *"God is not a man, that He should lie; nor a son of man, that He should repent. Has He said, and will He not do? Or has He spoken, and will He not make it good?"*

> ISAIAH 55:8 *"For My thoughts are not your thoughts, nor are your ways My ways," says the Lord."*

Unfortunately, some preachers have told congregations that what they say is what God says. It would be truthful if they would give credit to God, for inspiring them through the Word. Christians are ambassadors for Christ; we don't speak on our own behalf, but on the behalf of the One who sent us. Be aware, preachers who never give God credit for His own work, are not true. They seek to be people pleasers only, not pleasing God. They only want to make a "name" for themselves. Power and money are the girth of their intentions.

Three problems with men and churches who claim that a man can be pope are: the problem of preaching against marriage, supporting homosexuals to get their money, and the fact that they give money to the homeless, keeping them homeless. According to Hebrews 13:4, marriage is honorable and the Bible speaks on being wary of ministers, who discourage others on getting married. No one should be punished or found unfit, just because they got married. It does not take away from their ministry, but makes it better. Jesus never encouraged these evil things.

9. Does forgive and forget go together?
Answer: No. Luke 17:3.

> VERSE 3 *"Take heed to yourselves. If your brother sins against you, rebuke him; and if he repents, forgive him."*

Evil men and imposters will say just forgive and forget. According to Jesus' Word, He says if they repent, forgive them. If they don't repent, they are not forgiven. The word "if" implies a lot.

When people say "forgive and forget," it's like they think God is ignorant. For example, they probably think that God should allow the devil back into the Kingdom of Heaven, even though he never repented. It's like telling God that what the devil did was in the past, and He should just get over it, even though the devil is still presently challenging Christians. The forget part of their forgiveness, is not part of the repenting way. Forgetting something has to do with going on with your life, after you confront the problems in your life. The whole point of repenting is recognizing the wrong that you do, and changing that behavior to match the standards that God has set. They can't forget something, until the bad behavior is stopped!

10. Are men supposed to cry?
Answer: Yes. John 11:35 "Jesus wept." Romans 12:15.

ROMANS 12:15 *"Rejoice with those who rejoice, and weep with those who weep."*

Some men see crying as a sign of weakness. Because women cry a lot, in general, they see women as being weak, and letting their emotions control them. In reality, the ones who don't let out their emotions, in some constructive way, are the ones who are weak. If a man cries, he is seen as acting like a woman. Of course, as we gain maturity, by going through the pains of life, or "fire," there is a time to cry, and a time to not cry. You know the difference by the Anointing of God that teaches you.

If a person sees crying as weakness, it means that person

is not in touch with himself or herself. You have to let out frustration and anger in some meaningful way. Crying is one of those ways. Some men resort to violence, or promiscuous behavior. They let their anger out in the most ineffective way. Some get drunk, and some hold their anger in, which causes not only spiritual problems, but physical problems.

Crying is just an outlet that God has given us, in order to alleviate some of our spiritual stress. If we don't use the gift, we are helping to ruin ourselves, because that sadness ends up controlling the way we treat people, how we work, and it could cause medical problems, like cancer. If a man wants to grow education-wise, he has to conquer the "demons" of the past, in order to move on with a bright and prosperous future. It is ineffective to try and run away from them or try to hide them. I've seen some men try to run away from paying their child support payments, and have to run away forever; never being able to keep a decent job, or career, for fear of being incarcerated or never having enough money to sustain a living.

Some people grow up believing that emotions are bad, but it's not the emotions, it's the sin. If people would obey God, they wouldn't have to deal with so many problems, caused by doing evil. Emotions are good, because they show us that we are human, and we know if something is good or bad.

Jesus is God, but He's also a human example of a very powerful man, crying. He was not ashamed of showing His emotions, because it conveyed the power and compassion of His heart. In the Scripture given in John 11, Jesus was visiting a family in Bethany who had lost a brother. Jesus showed how much He loved Lazarus, the deceased, and later He did raise Lazarus from the dead. Christians allow themselves to show emotion, but they also keep the hope that all is not lost. Sorrow is temporary for those who trust in God. It is okay that men cry, because it means that the heart is not hardened by the calamities of life. It shows compassion of heart.

11. Are Christians supposed to judge?
Answers: Yes. John 7:24; Matthew 7:1-5; Corinthians 6:1-3.

JOHN 7:24 *"Do not judge according to appearance, but judge with righteous judgment."*

MATTHEW 7:1-5 *"Judge not, that you be not judged. 2 For with what judgment you judge, you will be judged, and with the measure you use, it will be measured back to you. 3 And why do you look at the speck in your brother's eye, but do not consider the plank in your own eye? 4 Or how can you say to your brother, "Let me remove the speck from your eye"; and look, a plank is in your own eye? 5 Hypocrite! First remove the plank from your own eye, and then you will see clearly to remove the speck from your brother's eye."*

According to Scripture, it might seem as if Jesus is contradicting Himself, but in reality, both passages of Scripture are saying the same thing. When Matthew 7:5 says, "And then you will see clearly to remove the speck from your brothers' eye," this is the same as judging with righteous judgment. God never contradicts Himself.

The important thing is not to judge by appearance, because appearances can be deceiving. Christians judge by the truth, which is righteous judgment. The Bible is the truth, the gospel of Jesus Christ. If children of God never judged anything, we would be as everyone else who, unfortunately, does judge by looks only, not by merit. Some think that good is bad and bad is good; they write songs, books, plays, etc., about how they believe love did them wrong, when really it was their own sins that did it. Love is good, it never does wrong; lust is actually what people allow to lead them astray. If people don't believe in judging, then they're not considering even the Book of Judges, which is a part of the Bible. Judging is a daily routine that's normal, but the truth is our guide. When people really embrace making righteous judgment, it actually has an opposite effect; you end up judging less, when you realize that you don't know everything or everyone's situation. One of the descriptions of Christians, is that we're quiet. It has a humbling effect when you realize your own faults, compared to others.

As far as differences are concerned, John 7 is speaking to Christians and Matthew 7 is speaking to hypocrites. Jesus cautions everyone who hears Him to not judge by appearance, but the truth. Hypocrites are very good at watching everyone else, but not watching their own actions. Jesus warns them in verse 5. The only way to really judge, is with the Lord God leading which is what sincere Christians practice.

12. Are you "backsliding" back into sin, if you don't go to church every Sunday?

Answers: No. Romans 10:9-13; Hebrews 10:24-25; Proverbs 14:14; Jeremiah 2:19.

> HEBREWS 10:24-25 "And let us consider one another, in order to stir up love and good works, 25 not forsaking the assembling of ourselves together, as is the manner of some, but exhorting one another, and so much the more, as you see the Day approaching."
>
> PROVERBS 14:14 "The backslider in heart will be filled with his own way, but a good man will be satisfied from above."
>
> JEREMIAH 2:19 "Your own wickedness will correct you, and your backslidings will rebuke you. Know therefore, and see that it is an evil and bitter thing that you have forsaken the Lord your God, and the fear of Me is not in you," says the Lord God of hosts.

Some people who put others down, because they don't always go to "church," are people who believe that the church is a building. They really don't believe that the church is flesh. Look at Colossians 1:24-29. They really don't believe that they are the temple of the Holy Spirit, which is spoken in the Word. They don't understand spiritual things, at all.

Secondly, the reason there is choppiness with the attendance of some, because some churches are being led by people who are against Christ. The Bible specifically gives instructions to turn away from those types of people (2 Timothy 3:5). That particular church becomes secular or a type of cult. Christians do not involve themselves with churches that practice sin, or give into behavior that is not led by love. Some are going through a rite of passage, like Jesus did; going into the "wilderness," to be tempted. Jesus didn't start his ministry until He was about 30. It's important to be committed, but not led by frivolous regulations (Galatians 3). Because Jesus died on the Cross for our sins, we are no longer bound by ungodly rules, or human restrictions.

Backsliding means an act of turning from God, after conversion. Attendance of church and backsliding, are two different things. Because, spiritually speaking, Christians are the Church; they always attend church within themselves. Backsliding has to do with not being moral. For example, the reason some people continue to defile their bodies, by smoking cigarettes, is because they don't allow themselves to be convinced by God's love, and stop. Some people think that speaking love is good enough, but God also looks for action; people who hear the Word, from the Bible, and do it!

13. ARE WOMEN SUPPOSED TO PREACH?
Answers: Yes. Joel 2:28; Acts 2:17.

ACTS 2:17 *"And it shall come to pass in the last days, says God, that I will pour out of My Spirit on all flesh: your sons and your daughters shall prophesy, your young men shall see visions, your old men shall dream dreams."*

The oppression of women is such an old tradition. In the past, women were physically restrained, with violence, from learning. Men did not think it necessary for a woman to learn how to read. Many third world countries still believe this. Men and women who are in disbelief that

God could give His Word to a woman is caused by two reasons. One reason has to do with the fact that they think Eve brought sin into the world, and secondly, because they are confused about 1–Corinthians 14:34-36, among other Scriptures. This is what it says:

> "Let your women keep silence in the churches: for it is not permitted unto them to speak; but they are commanded to be under obedience, as also saith the law. And if they will learn anything, let them ask their husbands at home: for it is a shame for women to speak in the church. What? came the word of God out from you? or came it unto you only?"

God never contradicts Himself. It has been expressed that the Corinthian Church may have had some issues. In the last verse 36, obviously some of their women had some arrogance, and did not have the truth on their side They were being punished! Verse 34 of chapter 14 said it using the pronoun "your" in conjunction with women, meaning the women of the Corinthian Church. The pronoun "your" is possessive here. Whatever was going on, we do know that there are differences between how men and women learn. The reason there are misunderstandings sometimes between sexes is because, men bring the technical (facts and figures), and women bring comprehension or understanding. One day I was listening to a chef at a Sears department store say, "Words are for women, pictures are for men." He said it very simply, and truthfully.

When Jesus was on the earth, He understood this very well. For the men, He gave them a picture of what love was. Jesus showed through His actions how to love, because it is documented by the Bible that the men had trouble understanding what He was saying, the parables. Even after Jesus was crucified on the Cross, He was kind and came back to show Himself to the men, so they could see that everything He said was true. With the women, Jesus spoke. Because He was speaking love, they understood. Women understand love better because of the Genesis experience; because Eve gained wisdom. Men are very good at speaking love, and women are very good at doing love. In retrospect, to be balanced through Jesus, men need to work on doing love. When the men learn how to do love, the women will be able to speak love. Jesus is a balancer, a mediator. Both men and women have maturity but in different aspects of life. Men are more mature in visually technical things and women are more mature in motive, being critical thinkers. Men like to get only bits and pieces of a story, but women like to get the whole story. Another way to state the differences of men and women: men are like knowledge, and women are like comprehension. Women help men understand what they have. Women get knowledge from their husbands and men get wisdom from their wives. There's a balance because, in the Christian home, each helps the other to grow in the knowledge of love, through Jesus' example.

Women preachers are very much needed, in order to help the family grow in the knowledge of the Law of Kindness (Proverbs 31). Women are not to command men but, according to Proverbs 1:8, give the law. God calls both men and women to preach the Gospel of Jesus Christ, which is of peace.

About Family

14 DOES THE BIBLE SAY THAT IT'S OKAY TO SPANK CHILDREN?
Answer: No. Romans 1:30; Proverbs 13:24; Isaiah 11:1; Proverbs 14:3; Psalms 34:21; Isaiah 53:9.

ISAIAH 11:1 "There shall come forth Rod from the stem of Jesse, and a Branch shall grow out of his roots."

PROVERBS 13:24 "He who spares his rod hates his son, but he who loves him disciplines him promptly."

14:3 "In the mouth of a fool is a rod of pride, but the lips of the wise will preserve them."

ROMANS 1:30 "Backbiters, haters of God, violent, proud, boasters, inventors of evil things, disobedient to parents."

ISAIAH 53:9 "And they made His grave with the wicked, but with the rich at His death, because He had done no violence, nor was any deceit in His mouth."

People who believe that God condones violence against children, are misinformed people. If they would only study the Word in the Bible, they would find out that "rod" is not used in the literal sense, here. For example, Proverbs 14:3 speaks of the rod of pride. Pride is one of those spiritual things, like an idea, because we've never seen it; it's comparable to the wind; but we know pride exists, because we see the results of it. It can be damaging if used improperly. Romans 1:30 speaks on how God is wrathful against violent people. God has never supported people who hit their children, in any way. Jesus was not violent.

The reason some people believe in disciplining their children with violence, is because it's how they were raised. They have been persuaded that it works, because if it was good for them, it's good for their children. The problem with that thinking, these adults are not all right. Spanking sometimes works temporarily, but it leaves permanent scars. It teaches that if someone doesn't do what you want, hit them. It causes discouragement. Besides teaching children how to be violent, it also causes children to have an inferiority complex. This type of abuse actually lowers the IQ of kids. It inhibits their mind in learning. They believe it's how they're supposed to be treated, because in some way, it's their fault, which is certainly not true. God is love; He does not hurt His children. It's like they're being punished for being born. They're not being encouraged to love, live, and be successful. Their success is temporary, and they never really find true love, because they don't allow God to teach them self-love. If you don't know how to love yourself, you can't love others, in the proper way. Imagine being on an airplane, and the pressure in the cabin is low on oxygen. Before you can help anyone else with their oxygen mask, you have to put your mask on, first. You can't help anyone if you're dead!

RELATED SCRIPTURE:
>COLOSSIANS 3:21 *"Fathers, do not provoke your children, lest they become discouraged."*

Fathers are warned in not angering their children, because fathers are the "heads." If daddy loves, mommy can be a lover to daddy and to the children. Children will love themselves, and other people of the world. Everyone is influenced by fathers; they are so needed in the family life, just as mothers are. Many times, the reason mothers are violent or verbally abusive, is because they're getting no love. It's physically and mentally too stressful to take on being both a father and mother, for fatherless children. A woman is not capable of such a task. So, God focuses on fathers, because the woman is not the "head." How the husband treats the wife, influences the way she responds to certain situations. In war there is violence, but the family can't function properly if it is ruled with violence, instead of love.

15. Are children to be respected?
Answer: Yes. 1 Peter 5:1-7.

1 PETER 5:1-7 "The elders who are among you I exhort, I who am a fellow elder and a witness of the sufferings of Christ, and also a partaker of the glory that will be revealed: 2 shepherd the flock of God which is among you serving as overseers, not by compulsion but willingly, not for dishonest gain but eagerly; 3 nor as being lords over those entrusted to you, but being examples to the flock; 4 and when the Chief Shepherd appears, you will receive the crown of glory that ""does not fade away. 5 Likewise you younger people, submit yourselves to your elders. Yes,

all of you be submissive to one another, and be clothed with humility, for God resists the proud, but gives grace to the humble, 6 therefore humble yourselves under the mighty hand of God, that He may exalt you in due time, casting all your care upon Him, for He cares for you."

Verse 5 speaks on both elders and youth being obedient or submissive to each other. In the Christian family, we don't believe in belittling people, whatever their age. Everyone has something to offer to the family, even the youngest one. Children are an inheritance to be cherished. The reason some old or young misbehave is because they are not being respected. Respect is a part of the definition of love.

16. WAS MARY, THE MOTHER OF JESUS, A SAINT?

Answer: No. Matthew 10:34-39; 12:46-50; Mark 3:31-35; Luke 8:19-21; Hebrews 13:5; John 7:1-9; Isaiah 53:3.

MATTHEW 12:46-50 "While He was still talking to the multitudes, behold, His mother and brothers stood outside, seeking to speak with Him. 47 Then one said to Him, 'Look, Your mother and Your brothers are standing outside, seeking to speak with You.' 48 But He answered and said to the one who told him, 'Who is My mother and who are My brothers?' 49 And He stretched out his hand toward His disciples and said, 'Here are my mother and my brothers! For whoever does the will of My Father in heaven, is My brother and sister and mother.' "

RELATED SCRIPTURES:

HEBREWS 13:5 "Let your conduct be without covetousness; be content with such things as you have. For He Himself has said, 'I will never leave you nor forsake you.'"

ISAIAH 53:3 "He is despised and rejected by men, A man of sorrows and acquainted with grief. And we hid, as it were, our faces from Him; He was despised; and we did not esteem Him."

We know that Joseph, Mary's husband was not Jesus' real father, because Mary was a virgin. Jesus' brothers were accounted for in John 7:1-9 as not believing in him. But according to what Jesus said in Matthew, Mark and Luke, not even his mother believed in her own son. She served as the best incubator to usher Jesus into the world, but he never included her as being His family. She was included with her other sons, as not hearing the Word of God, and not doing it. If they had been a part of His family, He would have greeted them. I can feel the pain that Jesus felt, knowing that they rejected Him. The Scriptures rightly say, "He was a man of sorrows, acquainted with grief."

In Hebrews 13:5 and other passages of Scripture, we read how Jesus will never leave us, or forsake us. It seems as if Jesus was forsaking His mother and brothers. On the contrary, they had forsaken Him. One of the things believers know, if Jesus was in the flesh and walking around, He would not ignore His saints. Christians are saints; we are the real Jews, who are discussed in the book of Romans, in Chapter 10. We were sanctified after the blood borne; Jews rejected their own Savior. God blessed us to take their inheritance as children of God to glory, in Heaven. Of course, we see that some of the Jews have become Christian. Whoever confesses, with their mouth, the Lord Jesus, and believes in their heart that God raised Him from the dead, shall be saved. (Romans 10:9) Whoever you are, you are saved, Jew or Gentile.

Mary loved what Jesus could do, but was lacking in love for who He was. Those who are rich are classic examples of people who may not know who their real friends are. But all of us have to, at some point in our lives, give up bad habits and bad people. We all need encouraging and loving people to live out our days, even in Heaven. Sad and disturbing to say, on three different accounts, in Scripture, Jesus did not include Mary as being a member of His family. Because we know that Jesus cares about His saints, He would not have ignored them, but would have greeted them. According to Jesus' words and actions, we see that Mary was not a saint.

One of the pains of being a Christian is finding out who your family is, and who is not. Jesus plainly stated that His family is those who hear the Word of God, meaning understand, and do it, as Luke 8:19-21 says. In my own personal family experiences, I see what Jesus was going through, personally. He went through a mourning process, just like all Christians do. We go through what He went through, in our own unique way. It is overwhelmingly hard to come to grips with the fact that the family you were born into is not really your family, spiritually.

17. Does God support homosexuality?
Answer: No. Romans 1:18-32.

VERSES 18-32 *"For the wrath of God is revealed from heaven against all ungodliness and unrighteousness of men, who suppress the truth in unrighteousness, 19 because what may be known of God is manifest in them, for God has shown it to them. 20 For since the creation of the world, His invisible attributes are clearly seen being understood by the things that are made, even his eternal power and Godhead, so that they are without excuse, 21 because, although they know God, they did not glorify Him as God, nor were thankful, but became futile in their thoughts, and their foolish hearts were darkened. 22 Professing to be wise, they become fools, 23 and changed the glory of the incorruptible God into an image made like corruptible man, and birds and four-footed animals and creeping things. 24 Therefore God also gave them up to uncleanness in the lusts of their hearts, to dishonor their bodies among themselves, 25 who exchanged the truth of God for the lie, and worshiped and served the creature rather than the Creator, who is blessed forever. Amen.*

26 For this reason God gave them up to vile passions. For even their women exchanged the natural use for what is against nature. 27 Likewise also the men, leaving the natural use of the woman, burned in their lust for one another, men with men com-

mitting what is shameful, and receiving in themselves the penalty of their error, which was due. 28 And even as they did not like to retain God in their knowledge, God gave them over to a debased mind, to do those things which are not fitting; 29 being filled with all unrighteousness, sexual immorality, wickedness, covetousness, maliciousness full of envy, murder, strife, deceit, evil-mindedness; they are whisperers, 30 backbiters, haters of God, violent, proud, boasters, inventors of evil things, disobedient to parents, 31 undiscerning, untrustworthy, unloving, unforgiving, unmerciful 32 who, knowing the righteous judgment of God, that those who practice such things are deserving of death, not only do the same, but also approve of those who practice them."

RELATED SCRIPTURES:

PROVERBS 1:8 "My son, hear the instruction of thy father, and forsake not the law of thy mother. 9 For they shall be an ornament of grace unto thy head, and chains about thy neck."

EXPLANATION: This passage of scripture speaks the truth very clearly, God does not agree with the behavior of some who gravitate toward the homosexual lifestyle, but what I will do next, is explain why. To help me explain why, Ephesians 5:28 will aid me:

"So husband ought to love their own wives as their own bodies; he who loves his wife, loves himself."

The scripture in Ephesians enlightens us on the fact, when a husband loves his wife he loves himself, but when a man says that he is gay, it lets us know that he does not love her, and he does not love himself. Some homosexuals say Christians are the ones who hate, but they're wrong. True Christians always love. We also know the Scripture which says, we wrestle not against flesh and blood. . . . If a person is a true Christian, it means they are not violent.

Every person who longs for a companionship type of relationship with another human being wants to be with someone who is comparable with him, or her. Woman was made from man and therefore, they make a perfect match. The problem that gays face is the fact that they believe God made a mistake. Some of them think they are a man trapped in a woman's body or a woman trapped in a man's. They hate being a man or they hate being a woman. They have much insecurity and low self-esteem, and it produces either hate for all women, or hate for all men. There's nothing wrong with either. We all have the sin condition, and need to go through Jesus the Christ to be saved from it. The "it" that I speak of is our constant tendency to hate the creation that God created, including us. The hate that homosexuals believe in, is one of the reasons God does not support their ways.

Another reason has to do with the sanctity of the family. The Scripture in Proverbs 1:8, speaks on how sons get instructions from fathers, and the Law from their mothers. The law they learn is the law of kindness. But when homosexuals become couples, the children they have will not get this balance in the home. Each parent, male and female, has a special role in the development of a child. Without this stability, children are confused. I speak mostly of gays and not lesbians, because if men obey God, the women will follow. It's not something that we made happen, but it is the natural working of things. Men always lead, whether they know it or not. The homosexual women are, because the men are. The self-hatred started with the men, not the women. Men, understand how powerful you are!

18. Does Jesus' lineage include African people?
Answer: Yes. Matthew 1:1-17; Ruth 4:18-22; Luke 3:23-38.

MATTHEW 1:1-17 "The book of the genealogy of Jesus Christ, the Son of Abraham: 2 Abraham begot Isaac, Isaac begot Jacob, and Jacob begot Judah, and his brothers, 3 Judah begot Perez and Zerah by Tamar, Perez begot Hezron, and Hezron begot Ram. 4 Ram begot Amminadab, Amminadab begot Nahshon, and Nahshon begot Salmon. 5 Salmon begot Boaz by Rahab, Boaz begot Obed by Ruth, Obed begot Jesse, 6 and Jesse begot David the king. David the king begot Solomon, by her who had been the wife of Uriah. 7 Solomon begot Rehoboam, Rehoboam begot Abijah, and Abijah begot Asa. 8 Asa begot Jehoshaphat, Jehoshaphat begot Joram, Joram begot Uzziah. 9 Uzziah begot Jotham, Jotham begot Ahaz, and Ahaz begot Hezekiah. 10 Hezekiah begot Manasseh, Manasseh begot Amon, and Amon begot Josiah. 11 Josiah begot Jeconiah, and his brothers about the time, were carried away to Babylon. 12 And after they were brought to Babylon, Jeconiah begot Shealtiel, and Shealtiel begot Zerubbabel. 13 Zerubbabel begot Abiud, Abiud begot Eliakim, and Eliakim begot Azor. 14 Azor begot Zadok, Zadok begot Achim, and Achim begot Eliud. 15 Eliud begot Eleazar, Eleazar begot Matthan, and Matthan begot Jacob. 16 Anchacob begot Joseph, the husband of Mary, of whom was born Jesus, who is called Christ. 17 So all the generations from Abraham to David are fourteen generations, and from the captivity in Babylon, until the Christ, are fourteen generations.

EXPLANATION: To help us with Jesus' lineage, I want to start by focusing on four women: Tamar, Rahab, Ruth and Bathsheba, the wife of Uriah. All four of these women were descended from Ham, one of Noah's sons, who were from the African continent, in the countries of Ethiopia and Egypt. Cush is another name for Ethiopia. Tamar and Rahab were Canaanites, Ruth was a Moabite, and Bathsheba is believed to have been Hittite. The Moabites are mentioned in Genesis 19:37; they are descended from Abraham's nephew, Lot. The name Moabite means black. The Hittites are referenced in Genesis 23:10-20. Ham was one of the sons who repopulated the earth, after God had destroyed it by the Flood. All of the offspring Ham had was: Cush, Mizraim, Put, and Canaan. Some nations were identified by the offsprings' names. In 2000 BC, the original inhabitants of Canaan were forced out, because of their pagan religion, by the Israelites, whom God promised the land. (The references are Genesis 10:6-20 and Genesis 12:5-6.)

Many people, who study the story of Noah, remember that Ham's son Canaan was cursed by Noah, because when Noah was drunk and asleep uncovered, Ham looked at his Father's naked body, which was seen as a dishonor. The reason Ham looked was most likely because of the visual and hands-on talent he had, being the youngest. Black people are the "Baby," which includes being the natural artists of the family. The other brothers helped to cover him up. When Noah found out what happened, he cursed Canaan, because of his Father and his descendants would be servants to the descendants of Shem and Japheth. (Ham's immoral behavior is noted in Genesis 9:22-25.)

In the order of their births, Japeth is the eldest. He is the ancestor who occupied both Asia Minor and Europe. (The reference is Genesis 10:2-5. Shem is the middle child. He is the ancestor of the Semitic people who include: Jews, Armenians, Persians, Assyrians, and the Arabians. (The reference is Genesis 10:22-32.) Queen of Sheba comes from Arabia, for example, and she was African! The Arabian people are from the Middle East, which means they are descended from Ishmael. Ishmael was the son Abraham had with his second wife Hagar; she was also Egyptian. Abraham was descended from Shem. Read Genesis 16 for more on the situation with Abraham, Hagar and Ishmael.

The relevance of knowing Jesus' lineage is to have an understanding of the truth. For so many years, the offsprings of Japheth have lied to many people, about Jesus' ethnic background. They have always claimed He was Caucasian, or White, but in reality, He was of a darker

About Family

color of an African. When they want people to believe their version of history; they commit the sin of blasphemy, because they use the lie to oppress people; it includes the sin of bearing false witness. It tries to make God look bad, when people who claim to be of Him, and are not. The information that was withheld has hurt many people, and the minds of many are still oppressed, as a result of the lie. For example, many of the Mexican Indians are still persuaded in thinking that Jesus was blond haired and blue eyed, because it's what they've been taught. In most churches, they show a picture of a White Jesus, hanging above their sanctuary. They avoid the truth, because they know that some of their congregants are very racist, and will leave if they admit the truth of Jesus' ethnicity. They will take their money with them. They don't want that! It is easy to deceive people when they don't know the truth; they don't have any positive pride. They always see themselves as inferior, which we know has happened in the African-American or Black community here in America, and around the world. The descendants of Japheth did not want the world to know that Jesus was born through African women; of course, including Mary. She is a member of Ham's side of the family. The history of Japeth is angering, but if there's repentance there's forgiveness.

African descendant people have been discriminated against, all because of the lie. Many effects include medical maltreatments and discrimination, especially against Black women; leading to hatred of their own appearance (Black men against Black women), and the phenomenon of the generational curse of ignorance, and poverty. These things still happen and need to be remedied. In the end though, we see how the curse of Noah, ends up being a blessing for Ham's descendants.

The medical maltreatment of Black women has led to many deaths of children. According to the office of Minority Health, African-Americans have 2.3 times the infant mortality rate as non-Hispanic, whites. The infant mortality rate is highest among African-American families, because people of that race believe in too many stereotypes, concerning them. They think that Black women are the strongest, but in reality we are the most fragile. Even the hair on our heads breaks the easiest! The only reason African people have survived is because God has given a promise. We see that the promise God gave was Jesus

The second issue is the fact that some Black men discriminate against their own Black women. The conditional love they were raised to believe in fails them. In order for them to realize the power of unconditional love, they would have to acknowledge the omniscience and omnipotence of God. These men have to believe they are good enough in order to avoid destroying their own identity and seed. Ezra 9:1-2 speaks about how the Jews had made the same mistake of being unfaithful to God by intermarrying with Pagans and mingling their holy race. But now, African-Americans are the slaves. God delivered us from the physical slavery and now we are in need of being delivered from the mental slavery. Being chosen by God also puts us in the position of making sure we don't mingle our holy blood with those who do not comprehend God's love. Genesis 24:4 gives us proof that God wants his children to stay within their own people. Some think having a mixed-race relationship proves they are not prejudiced, but it actually proves they are. It's okay to be African-American and enjoy or be involved with other cultures and races of people. Our uniqueness makes us each powerful. Because of the lie, many still believe they will not be accepted having Black women for wives. They feel they will be more successful marrying Asian or Caucasian women; Japheth's descendants. It's the old Adam and Eve situation, where the woman is being blamed for what the man has done. We see how some Black men blame their women for being unhappy, which in turn, causes them to go to other races of women to be satisfied, and even be married. These other women have to remember, Black women come from Black men. The man who hates his wife, hates himself. It is hard for a man to love others, if he can't even love himself. Secondly, it disrupts the development of the children, because they automatically are taught prejudice against the races, believing in stereotypes, and they also have self-identity problems. Problems come with the "territory," because most Black men, in this situation, are just having vengeance against Black women, which means there is a lack of love, and the other women, are being spitefully used. Of course, a Christian woman need not worry about being blessed with her husband, because God always provides for His own daughters. Tamar, Rahab, Ruth and Bathsheba were all blessed with their Black husbands! In these days and times, though, if a woman of any race wants to have some reassurance that her husband really loves her, it is good to refer back to the first section of the book. 1 Thessalonians 4, is the key. Stop being the harlot and obey God by not having pre-marital sex; in 1 John 4:1-6, the passage of Scripture speaks on testing the spirits. If you want to find out how committed and how much self-control a man has, let God help you. Listen to His Word and obey Him, because He knows men, more than anyone. 1 Kings 11 gives more evidence that God wants his children to not commit incest, but Nehemiah 13:23-27, especially verse 25 gives the actual law as it pertains to intermarriage. Deuteronomy 7 and Exodus 34 give also the law against intermarriage and Ezra 10 gives instructions on the repentance of those who have sinned this sin of unfaithfulness to God. The incest I speak of has to do with the three races being siblings. Some think that means if their children are half and half that they will be smarter, but it does not. They may excel with rote memorization, but have trouble having original thoughts. Some of the children have actual medical issues because of the incest; their lives are automatically at risk because of their parents' sins. It is child endangerment.

The third issue is the phenomenon of the generational curse of ignorance, and poverty; which also stems off of the lie that causes people to think that God has forsaken them, because they're not White. Fathers and mothers are the foundation for their children, because they lead the way, by example. Because many of the children have no stable examples of Godly progress and success, it is hard for them to see themselves as having a bright and prosperous future in love and happiness. The boys grow up not being able to be trustworthy in relationships, making it impossible to propose marriage. It is the mother's job to nurture her son; it is the father's job to instruct. But if the son only has his mother, he's not being instructed, he is being spoiled, because of his mother's guilt. In some cases the mother becomes the opposite for fear of ruining him, and ends up being an unloving parent; never giving hugs, praise, and always yelling. This is partly the reason some Black boys go to other races of women, for comfort. They end up generalizing all Black women and being repelled by them. When I say generalizing, I mean they become prejudiced against their own selves. It is self-hatred. The girls who are always overly critical of themselves, become too "hard-core," and insensitive. In many cases, it's as if the girls are being raised to work, and the boys are being raised not to work. The girls are being instructed but never nurtured. They also suffer, because they are not being raised with their fathers.

The fact that many believe that Jesus was White has caused much confusion. Other races of people think it's okay to discriminate against African people because they see them as inferior. The existence of God's Son Jesus, gives African people hope that the "servant" is first in God's sight. As Jesus said, "The first shall be last and the last first." A passage of Scripture that gives us more insight is the Song of Solomon 1:1-6. It reads as follows:

> "The song of songs, which is Solomon's. 2 Let him kiss me with the kisses of his mouth: for thy love is better than wine. 3 Because of the savor of thy good ointments, thy name is as ointment poured forth, therefore do the virgins love thee. 4 Draw me, we will run after thee: the king hath brought me into his chambers: we will be glad and rejoice in thee, we will remember thy love more than wine: the upright love thee. 5 I am black, but comely, O ye daughters of Jeru-

salem, as the tents of Kedar, as the curtains of Solomon. 6 Look not upon me, because I am black, because the sun hath looked upon me: my mother's children were angry with me; they made me the keeper of the vineyards; but mine own vineyard have I not kept." (King James Version of the Bible)

EXPLANATION: Solomon, who himself was descendant from Ham, is believed to have written this, because his name is in it. It describes a Shulamite woman, and her love for her husband. It also describes the fact that she is Black, and her brothers and sisters are jealous. They're so jealous that they made her a servant, in their vineyards. They have made things hard for her, and we know this because she lets us know that she has not even kept her own vineyard. She's too busy being forced to keep theirs.

Kedar, the location she mentions, is a nomadic community in northern Arabia. It is known for its tents, which are woven from black goat's hair. It lets us know that this Shulamite woman is also Egyptian.

In certain versions of the Bible, the word describing the Shulamite woman, is the word dark. The writers of these versions try not to describe her as Black, or African, but tanned. They try to claim that she was dark, because she was working in the hot sun, in the fields. But the point is the fact that she describes her color as being darker than tan, and she is the servant of her siblings. Her ethnicity and degree of color are noted. I write this portion just to make people aware of the discrepancies that occurred because of racist attitudes. To this day, people see Africa as being so great that they continue to steal from the continent's resources, and violate the people.

The Scriptures show us that Jesus' lineage does include African people. The world treats Africa as the least, but God sees her as first. The fact that the majority of churches in America still showcase Jesus as White shows how people are still being led by fear. They don't want the truth, because it will show how superficial they are, and how much they reject Christ, the Son of God. They won't even accept his physical appearance, let alone the spiritual! Despite their ignorance, the Scriptures reassure us that God has never been racist. Jesus' lineage includes African people.

19. Is the use of psychology good or bad?
Answer: Bad. 2 Chronicles 7:12-14.

VERSES 12-14 "Then the Lord appeared to Solomon by night, and said to him, "I have heard your prayer; and have chosen this place for Myself as a house of sacrifice. 13 When I shut up heaven, and there is not rain, or command the locusts to devour the land, or send pestilence among My people, 14 if My people who are called by My name will humble themselves, and pray and seek My face, and turn from their wicked ways, then I will hear from heaven, and will forgive their sin, and heal their land."

As we know, psychology is the study of the human mind. What some do not know is, the reason many of us have anxiety is because of our sinful nature. All of our issues can be resolved with obedience to God. The reason we are blessed with the Bible, is so that we are protected from our own evil will. People in this field say that the person isn't bad, but it's just their actions. It represents how the head is always trying to blame the body for the sins; it is ironic because it perpetuates the theme of men blaming women, for their trouble. In that respect, psychology was very much created by men, not God. They don't understand that the actions are a reflection of that person; they are connected. The fact that they think there's a separation, only shows their ignorance, and denial of the human mind.

Three things that are wrong with psychology include: not being able to mention Jesus, blaming the victim, and using drugs to try to fix something that is spiritual. The fact that they shun mentioning the name of Jesus is a "telltale" sign that there is a rejection of God. When these counselors blame the victims for their hardship, it means they do not take into account Colossians 3:21, where God gives blame to fathers, for provoking their children to wrath, and discouraging them. They do not understand how powerful the father figure is in the lives of the family. If fathers obey God and love their families, there is order. The reason many people self-inflict pain and hurt others is because of this discouragement. The only way to fix it is through the understanding that the Bible gives, only through Jesus. He is our example of how to live life. I can imagine if Jesus were in the flesh with us today, some of the psychologists would try to give Him counseling for his sorrow. They would probably try to give Him a drug to control His mood swings, and depress his mind from thinking. The many drugs that people take have the same purpose, to block off the part of the brain that deals with emotion. What counselors don't understand, it is not emotion that makes people do evil, but the sinful nature. When love is introduced, everything falls into place. God's love is sufficient in healing the pains of the past, and giving peace to the mind. Psychology is a form of Gnosticism or false doctrine. It definitely gives terminology for the different issues of life, but only serves as manipulation. It's demonic because its origins are based on precepts that are not from the Gospel of Jesus Christ. Instead of leaning on God's understanding they lean on their own.

To The Reader

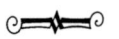

To my readers, I would like to introduce myself in order to testify to God's power in my life. Everyone has their own journey through which they believe God to work miracles. I don't just speak of God's love, but I show it. When you see me and read me, you are reading the Godly inspiration of a 33 year old virgin. I know from personal experience how it feels to be faithful.

In meekness and confidence of God's love, I share my heart's work with you so you will pass it on. Most think it's impossible for a woman to be faithful, but as an African-American woman God has groomed me in spiritual marriage, which has readied me for love with a future husband.

I give myself as an example, that it is possible to have real love. Not all women are whores! Do not give up on yourself being blessed and favored of God. Love and forgiveness of yourself is key. As time goes on, marinate in God's love and be powerful.